Copyright © 2019 by Cynthia Rawles

All rights reserved. This book or any portion thereof may not be reproduced or used in any manner whatsoever without the express written permission of the publisher. Please send such requests to: acmpublish@gmail.com

ISBN: 978-1-7329900-7-4

Printed by: A&C Marketplace Publishing LLP in the United States of America

SO, YOU THINK YOU WANT TO GET MARRIED?

CYNTHIA RAWLES

TABLE OF CONTENTS

Dedication	4
Acknowledgement	5
Introduction	6
Are **YOU** Ready?	10
Check Your Motives	15
The Importance of Waiting	19
What to Do While You Wait	25
Take Back Control	30
Take Yourself Off the Market	33
Don't Judge A Book	36
Do **YOU** Have What It Takes?	40
Imperfect Puzzle Pieces	44
Keep or Trade	49
Control Your Appetite	52
Repeat Offender – Cycle of Divorce	56
Don't Wait to Tell Me	60
Ready to Submit?	62
Keeping Your Own Grass Green	65
Happily Ever After	68
About the Author	71

DEDICATION

This book is dedicated to all couples; whether you're headed to the altar to say, "I Do" or you've already said "I Do!" This book is even for those that have said "I DO" but realized they no longer want to stay in this place. My prayer is that you gain a deeper relationship with the Father in order to fully understand your road together.

ACKNOWLEDGEMENT

A special thank you to Holy Spirit for the leading and guiding of such a writing project! He Rocks!

INTRODUCTION

WARNING! THIS BOOK IS FOR MATURE AUDIENCES ONLY! Put your seatbelt on because you're going for the ride of your life. Before we move any further, let's define the purpose of a seatbelt: *"A seatbelt, also known as a safety belt, is a vehicle safety device designed to secure the occupant of a vehicle against harmful movement that may result during a collision or a sudden stop. A seatbelt functions to reduce the likelihood of death or serious injury in a traffic collision by reducing the force of secondary impacts with interior strike hazards. A seatbelt applies an opposing force to the driver and passengers to prevent them from falling out or making contact with the interior of the car. Seatbelts are considered as Primary Restraint Systems (PRS), because of their vital role in occupant safety."* I believe that this manual will help guide and assist you in your decision-making process towards your next move from being single to saying; "I DO." Even if you're already married, maybe you didn't seek guidance which can cause you to feel as though you're treading on unfamiliar territory, but you're not alone. I pray that you allow this book to shed some light and bring a spark back to any dry places. Now that we have all passengers secured we can proceed! I'm getting in your car as your new driving instructor to ensure that you don't make any wrong turns and to ensure that you pay close attention to every curve and bump in the road; every red light, caution light, green light; every possible traffic signal and to make sure you stay in your lane. I want to make sure you see the counterfeit crossing in front of you, oops I mean pedestrians and hear every emergency vehicle coming your way. We will peel apart every traffic signal and apply it to marriage to make certain you grasp the meaning of this *lifelong* covenant agreement that God has ordained. This is a crucial time in your life and I'm here to make certain that you pass the written test as well as the road test. I believe, in order for change to take place, we must be bold enough to say what needs to be said. If you are sincere in the waiting period, we will give you some vital tools that will assist you while you wait. If you've already said; "I Do" this will also help you to endure the hardship and the uncertainties that are sure to show up. There are too many people making wrong decisions and sometimes those that make the right decisions abort too soon, so they never discover their true potential. We must learn how to discover each other and grow together!

As I become transparent in this book about my own struggles and success in marriage, my prayer is that you will find peace while you're waiting! Now, let me set the record straight, if you think that this book is about male bashing, name calling or putting all men in a certain category, you have the wrong perspective before you even begin. You've heard those negative words: *All men are dogs or they're no good men out here, etc.* Well, we've come to dispel those lies and to make sure you play your cards right and get your life in alignment with what a "good thing" looks like. What do I mean "good thing?" Proverbs 18:22 says; he who finds a wife finds a good thing and obtains favor of the Lord. You must get prepared and pampered like Esther so that you can be found.

In addition, you want your spouse to receive God's favor! Think about it this way, when you naturally trip or stumble over something your first impression is to look back to see what you've stumbled over right? I want you to be so ready for this position as a wife, that when he discovers you, it is the thing that he is willing to change for!

Marriage is like peeling an orange, it takes time, but every bite is sweeter and sweeter. I recently had a friend tell me that they didn't eat oranges. I inquired, and she told me that she didn't eat them because they took too much time and effort to peel. Well, this is exactly the attitude that we have concerning our marriages; we don't want to work at it! Just make certain that you're not the rotten fruit that will be picked over and tossed because of the bad smell, mold, mustiness or dry rot! You know, you've gone to the grocery store only to find stale fruit, undesirable to even take home. Well, not this time! Pay attention and take note and I believe that when you are picked out of the crowd, you will be a sweet-smelling fragrance, where the aroma is recognized everywhere the two of you go!

By now you are aware that I'm not here to change your mind about marriage, I've simply been sent to encourage you and to help you not only see outward but inward! This book is coming to you from 30 years of experience in this thing called marriage and I want to do my part in ensuring that you have the foreknowledge that you need to make sure you are ready and equipped before you say those most popular words; "I DO!" We want to make sure your first time around stays around FOREVER! It is also important to gain insight from other experienced couples that will help you succeed. I pray that as you read and submit to this teaching it will cause you to change if necessary, enhance if necessary, pull-in, fix-up, or whatever it will take so that you will be able to receive the desire of your heart in Christ Jesus. I am in no way trying to imply that looks are what's required. I'll explain later in another chapter in detail what I mean. But, in the meantime we have Esther as our example. Let's get ready to take this ride together!

ARE **YOU** READY?

Sounds a bit like a loaded question doesn't it? Before I move forward with this chapter, let us go to the dictionary. Webster defines the word "ready" as: *being prepared mentally or physically for some experience or action; prepared for immediate use.* Once I looked up this word, I stumbled across the adjectives associated which are: *Readier and Readiest!* Wow! Ok, Warning! I know this isn't good English so don't try to correct my language here; I'm going somewhere! Let's take the first word; Readier! *I'm going to be "Readier" than you! I'm going to be the "Readiest" in the building!* This should be your thought process. This should be your new mindset; Why? If you're in a room full of people, the eye of your future mate will be zoomed in on you and YOU alone! But, get this and hear me clearly, if you're not ready, HE WON'T SEE YOU! It won't matter what you have on or what you smell like. Yes, I know you're thinking, it worked for Esther. Yes, it did, but it took months for her to prepare herself. She sacrificed and was found in the place where she belonged. You could have purchased your finest apparel and the finest perfume, but a man seeking to find his "good thing" won't choose the wrong thing. So don't be envious or jealous of someone in the room that gets picked before you. I've heard the conversations and the questions asked; Why did he pick her? I'll answer it for you; SHE WAS READY! Now, the next question is; What does "Ready" look like? Before we get into what ready looks like, let's talk about what it does not look like. Now this could be one of the most disputed arguments but in my opinion "Ready" does not look like the shortest or tightest dress, the big hips and big thighs, the breast popping out of your blouse, the red bottom shoes, the most expensive car or the baddest house, how much money you have, the baddest weave, oops I mean hairstyle or the highest of degrees. Although appearance certainly matters, we all know that to be true. I'm just saying, don't let that be your bait because when you're uncovered, he will see the real you! However, when you put on the right fragrance and Godly character you will stand out amongst the crowd. Let's get out of this mindset that you're so desperate that you plan an attack by forging the bait, thinking that you can lure in your prey! When fishermen go out to fish, the bait that they use is usually dead, stinky or messy. Yes, we know that the fish will fall for the bait, but what do they do with it? They eat and when they are hungry again, they will search for more bait somewhere else. They are just hungry and are willing to accept what's given to them, although not completely satisfied. As we discussed, it's not about having material things and a bunch of stuff. The final question is; HOW READY ARE **YOU**?

Let's go back to Webster's definition mentioned above; *being prepared mentally or physically for some experience or action; prepared for immediate use.* When it's your turn, will you be immediately ready? Your right now answer will probably be; Yes! But wait, getting ready for anything takes time, patience, practice, evaluation, study, etc! Since we're talking about the opposite sex, let's go right to one of their favorite activities; sports. During football season it's amazing how the die-hard fans prepare for their upcoming games; the tailgate parties, rain or shine, etc. I can even image each team preparing as they watch videos of their opponent to scope out their strategies. Are you being watched or scoped out? This worlds' view on marriage seems to be so disjointed. We tend to have this illusion that by the time a person is a certain age they should have at least received a proposal, or they should be "hatched." Certainly, there is much hype in this arena. However, where is the hype on the preparation? I'm not saying that it is not anywhere to be found, I'm just questioning how readily available it is. I remember saying: "I DO" at such a young age. I was thinking about marriage even before I graduated from high school. Where could those thoughts have come from? Was I trying to justify the need to be sexually involved? Of course! I attached sexual intercourse with marriage, so no matter how young I was when I was introduced to sex, I thought marriage came along with it. When that didn't happen, and the relationship ended I felt as if I had given a part of me away only to be left empty, confused and depressed! I was too darn young to be thinking about marriage and the life-long journey I was headed for. But what do you think happened? I didn't get help so those emotions and urges never went away. I carried them over into the next relationship, not intentionally, maybe they just followed me. Where are the Naomi's? Naomi took Ruth under her wing as she was willing to go into unfamiliar territories, seeking God for her next. Ruth refused to let go. She chose to follow. Are you willing to follow, stay close and learn in order to run into success?

Before you say I DO, make sure you step back a bit, push the pause button, pray and evaluate every aspect. Treat this thing seriously, as if you're sitting down watching a video of this person you've chosen to spend the rest of your life with. Don't fall for the hype! Okay, he may come at you and tell you that you're the one, that's all well and good, but you need to take precaution and seek God on saying yes. I have a friend who received two proposals within two days and they both said that God told them that she was their wife! Okay, which was right? Take heed to the video because it shall become a clear glimpse of their life played out right before your eyes. It will show you how they've lived; what their childhood was like; how they were raised and by whom; whether their home was stable; how they treat their parents; working conditions or capabilities; revealed relationships; or if they have children or better yet, if they are taking care of their children? I'm not disputing the "love at first sight" theory, I'm just sending a warning to you to study and present your requests to God. All of these things are extremely vital and are not always discussed before the big day or sometimes not until many years later. Yes, you have this kind of control! Request a video from God your Father (Spirit of Discernment). He will reveal to you all of the hidden things. As a matter of fact, He will tell you if this is the one for you or not. As my Apostle would always encourage the singles to do; Ask God to remove you or them. Most people are afraid to do just that. I know for me I was afraid.

God showed me in a dream who my husband was going to be and I got so excited. I called him to tell him that he was going to be my husband only to hear *"I'm not getting married to anyone."* Wow! Did I hear right? Sure I did, I just left out the part where God told me Yes, but Wait! I totally ignored that part. I rushed into something that I was absolutely not prepared for. First of all, how in the world could I have been prepared when I had no real role models to pattern myself after? I lived in a single parent home and my neighborhood was full of single mothers with children, most had no fathers. There were men around but not steady. I remember my mom protecting me from some of those old goons! If there were any stable relationships, they must have been hidden. I had no Naomi to follow. No one was available, equipped or willing to teach me how to "Get Ready." Titus 2:4-5 says: *"That they may teach the young women to be sober, to love their husbands, to love their children, to be discreet, chaste, keepers at home, good, obedient to their own husbands, that the word of God be not blasphemed."*

Prepare and equip yourself NOW so that when he shows up YOU will be READY! These are questions to ponder on: Are you ready to be a helpmate? Are you ready to fulfill the assignment that God has for you? Are you willing to set aside selfish wants to please others? Are you ready to share your space? Are you ready to forego at times your own needs to fulfill the desire of others? Are you ready to cut back on frivolous, unnecessary spending? Are you ready to commit? Are you ready to put others before yourself? Are you ready to work hard? Are you ready to sacrifice? ARE YOU READY?

CHECK YOUR MOTIVES

Why do you want to get married? Yes, I asked the question! You may be wondering how someone who has been married for 30 years can ask such a question. Let me explain. If someone would have confronted me and asked me this simple question, just maybe, they would have heard my silence and my immaturity and took me to the school I call "wisdom and knowledge." As little girls we are raised to think about being a housewife and a mom. We play with the dolls and pretend they had husbands and children. We wore aprons while helping our moms cook in the kitchen. Well, some of us did! I credit my sisters with that part. I just wanted to eat and sleep. Back to the question at hand; why do you want to get married? Is it simply to justify those sexual desires that keeps lurking inside of you? Is it because you see others walking down-the-isle and you think it's your turn? Is it because your clock is ticking, and you don't want to be the only one on earth unmarried? Are you being forced by friends and family to tie the knot? Are you living together and want to put a sealed paper on it? Are you in a financial bind and you need support? Are you lonely? Are you trying to justify that he's yours? These questions can go on and on. Some of these can be valid questions. I was already in a sexual relationship, feeling as if I'd already given up the goods, so I thought; *"Why not seal this deal!"* I'm not saying that there is anything wrong with your answers to any of these questions. My goal here is to make sure you uncover the truth of your motives because in the revealing, you may discover why YOU attract the wrong type.

As a counselor and a coach, it is normal to hear questions concerning this very thing; *Why do we pick the wrong guy?* Let's evaluate this for a moment. Are you actually picking the wrong guy or are you attracting the wrong guy? I believe there is a difference. One must make sure "magnetic forces" are properly aligned so that you no longer attract the wrong type. Positive energy or good electricity can become a magnet. So, make sure you're not giving out negative vibes. Make sure your vibes don't smell like desperation! I'm not suggesting that you turn your noise up at offers that may come your way. I'm simply suggesting that you present yourself in a manner that will have them questioning who you are! You remember the song; Who's that lady? Don't be fooled by the "pickings." You know how you pick up fruit that appear to look healthy, but you get it home and find out it's rotten! At times, I've even found myself picking bad fruit because it was the last in the barrel and I was desperate for that particular type of fruit. Well, we don't want this to happen in your relationship. Examine your motives! Ask yourself the question; Am I desperate or can I wait on the right one?

There is a known scientific fact that two negative forces cannot connect, BUT two positives will pull together! THEY WILL CONNECT! What am I saying? If you're desperate, desperation will find you! It may initially look like you're connecting, but what have you connected to? Marriage is not some temporary fix that you jump into just to satisfy your desires, because certainly once the fix is fixed, or the hole is patched, it is only a matter of time before you see that maybe this wasn't all that it appeared to be! Especially if you're with the wrong one! Let's face it, marriage is certainly a challenge in itself, adding drama, wrong decisions, etc, to the mix won't make things better. And to be completely real here, after you've reached your climax, after the sexual high, whether you're hanging from the ceiling fans or the lights, you can't stay in this place all night, you will have to go to sleep. But what happens when you roll over the next morning and you look at this person next to you and you want to scream *"What have I done?"* Just like someone trying to fix a flat tire with fix-a-flat, after a while you are going to need something else for security and dependability. Driving long distance with fix-a-flat on your tires will yield some form of discomfort. You want to be able to travel with comfort, ease and relaxation, even in your marriage! Of course, you're going to hit bumps in the road but being with the one God has chosen for you will make the trip worth taking!

Let's talk about another possible motive - Your Appetite! If you are like me, I love to eat! Growing up on fried chicken, collard greens and potato salad didn't help much. Eating is a necessity, we must eat to live! Why is it suggested that we never go to the grocery store hungry or the buffet line? I'm glad you asked. It can cause you to overeat! If you're starving and you are at the buffet, you'll put any and everything on your plate, then you wonder why later on you feel sick to your stomach. Could it be that your eyes are bigger than your stomach, as we would say? Sometimes our appetite can be full of uncertainty, as it changes like the wind. In some cases, you desire everything you see, in other instances, we are selective. When it comes to food (relationships) sometimes we can't make up our mind. But in the moment of desperation we could eat (choose) everything in site. Sometimes we pick and choose the wrong stuff and realize later on that we can't handle those things. Food is heavy and too much of anything can cause major issues with our body. In the same manner, so can the wrong kind of relationship. 1 Corinthians 6:19-20 (NIV) says; *"Do you not know that your bodies are temples of the Holy Spirit, who is in you, whom you have received from God? You are not your own; you were bought at a price. Therefore honor God with your bodies."* We should look at this in the natural as well as the spiritual. How can you honor God with your body if you're putting anything in it or allowing anything to enter it? Some have said that they don't want marriage because it's too much work, but they would rather continue in a sinful, sexual relationship, thinking that there will be no consequences. Remember, a temporary fix won't work! At some point in your life your motives will need to change. Make sure you're not just desiring this type of "ministry" just because others are in it. You definitely don't know what their marriage/ministry entails. Don't go through life accepting just a temporary fix. Ask God to send your match. Examine your motives today!

THE IMPORTANCE OF WAITING!
W.A.I.T. (**W**hat **A**re you **I**n a hurry **T**o do)?

Why do I have to wait? I'm tired of being alone! I'm getting older and my needs are not being met! If these are some of the things that you're struggling with, stay with us! In today's society it is hard to minister to that single person that desires marriage, especially when you've been married for so long. But I come to tell you that the wait will be worth it! Okay, I hear you wondering; *How could she know that the wait is worth it when she has been married for so long and at such a young age?* To answer that; Yes, I married very young and if I knew half the things that I know now, I certainly would have prayed for the strength to wait. Now, let me tell you, I have a blessed married, but the struggle is real when you're not ready. I accepted Christ at a young age and was active in my church and the young adult choir; however, I did not have a personal relationship with the Father, I only knew of Him!

Where did the phrase "knowledge is power" come from? History says that this insight is at least four centuries old, formulated by philosopher Francis Bacon during the Enlightenment. But what does the bible say about it? The bible says; my people perish for a lack of knowledge. I was sinking, drowning, dying for a married mentor to show up in my life to tell me what I was supposed to do next. There had to be successful marriages somewhere, but where were they? The crazy thing about all of this was that my church was filled with married couples, but not one person felt led to share their experiences with me or to take me under their wing. When the announcement went out that I was getting married, one lady approached me and asked to see my ring; her comment was "Is that all you got?" She never offered to teach me anything about marriage. People seemed angry, as if they weren't happy for me and I never understood why. At this time in my young life I hadn't discovered what Titus 2:3-5 says, *"The aged women likewise, that they be in behaviour as becometh holiness, not false accusers, not given to much wine, teachers of good things; That they may teach the young women to be sober, to love their husbands, to love their children, To be discreet, chaste, keepers at home, good, obedient to their own husbands, that the word of God be not blasphemed."* I'm certain they knew, but the question remains; Why didn't they reach out to me to teach me? No one told me that I was too young. No one told me that I should wait. No one offered to give me tips. Oddly enough, the mentors that I did have, were successful single woman!

To my knowledge there weren't any real-talk types of books that would help me with the feelings that I was experiencing in the beginning. What were these feelings and emotions? Was this normal? Was it normal to be married and feel lonely and often wonder whether or not I made the right decision? Who could answer these questions for me? It took many years of trusting God in prayer and the stick and stay mentality that we were able to endure. So let me help you out a bit. I want to make sure you're not jumping into something just to get a quick fix as we talked about previously, because if you're not complete in your own personal relationship with Jesus you will look to man to fulfill those things and when they can't, *it's their fault*, at least that's what I believed! Unknowing to the both of us, the marriage road was certainly one that had to be traveled with much prayer. It was as if we had to get used to a new road construction that was coming to town. You know you've seen the road construction signs that warn you that there is a new traffic pattern or a warning of expected delays, you don't necessarily know what to expect, you just have to work through the changes or get accustomed to the detours. Some detours are good as they serve as warnings, but other detours can be a distraction, you must recognize and know the difference. I remember my sister was informed that her normal route to work was going to change for approximately one month. It caused a bit of anxiety as she didn't know what to expect. Well, it is the same in a marriage, we don't know what roads are in front of us and that can sometimes cause a bit of anxiety, but the exciting news is that as long as God is the center you'll eventually get back on the right road or the diverted road will lead you back to God! That's good news!

I remember when the state of Virginia opened up the inner loop and the outer loop. I didn't know which loop I was on for the most part. This is a great scenario of what "not waiting" looks like. When you're in a hurry to get married, it may seem glitzy and glamorous at first, but it would not be a good look if one day you're on the inner loop and he's on the outer loop *(going in different directions);* you're going clockwise and he's going counter clockwise! Somebody will be ready to take a detour or get off at the next exit because it looks safe. That's exactly what happened to me. I was so confused and uncertain about which "loop" I was on so I got off at the nearest exit and called for help. I was able to get help but what if help wasn't available (that relationship with Jesus)? Let's talk a bit about this exit. There are so many marriages that are being destroyed for various reasons, people aren't willing to fight for their marriages anymore. It becomes selfish reasons, one not getting their way or the other not being satisfied or whatever the case, so what happens, one or the other will find that exit that says; "come this way, you'll be safe here!" All exits aren't good exits. I remember traveling an area that I was not familiar with. Now the navigation told me that it should only take 20 minutes to get to my destination. Well, it took over an hour. What happened? I depended upon another source (voice) to tell me which way to go. This should not be in your marriage, leave the outsiders outside! Getting back to my trip; I was lost so I decided to take the next exit in hopes that I would be able to turn around and get a new start. Well, I took the next exit and I ended up in an area that I had never traveled. There were no signs to get me back to where I needed to be. There were hardly any street lights and all of the stores were closed so I could not stop and ask for directions. I finally had to ignore the navigation and pray. I eventually turned around and got back on track, but it took what seemed to be hours to find my way back. Don't allow this to happen in your marriage. Just wait! Just wait to be found! Even if he claims to have found the right one, you make sure for yourself that you ask the Lord to confirm that very thing. You never want to find yourself going in different directions.

W.A.I.T. In this instance, let's assume W.A.I.T. stands for "WHAT AM I THINKING?" Go ahead and ask yourself, What am I thinking? Are you thinking? Are you sure this is what you want? Are you ready to take on such a serious project? Yes, I said project! If you're not ready, it's okay! You may be good in the state of waiting! In this state, you could be waiting for maturity to take place; whether in you or your spouse or you could be waiting for the perfect timing of God. What if you decided that you couldn't wait any longer and you came up with a plan to go after your prey without waiting? Well, in counseling sessions I've encountered this attitude and in each instance, they indicated that they should have waited. 99.9999% (lol) of the time sex is the driving factor! Yep, I've been there! Hey, I should have waited too! I was certainly not ready to say, "I DO" but the thought of it was so attractive that I couldn't resist. As little girls, we think we prepare by playing house with dolls. Nope, that's not preparation at all! I was unnoticed, unprepared, uneducated, unskilled and uncovered and it almost caused me to go UNDER! There were absolutely no role models in my community that I could readily identify. The role model that I did have in my life was a successful professor who encouraged me throughout school. She worked at a local college where she encouraged me to pursue further education. She was single and had her own penthouse. I learned a lot from her but I never saw the relationship that I somehow knew she was hiding. So, what did I do? I acted just like the very thing that I was exposed to; the swing door policy! If one didn't show up I was available for the next one until they both collided! I knew I had to make a decision about my life quickly.

I was trying to fill a void, an empty space. The odd thing about this, I didn't know it was empty until I enjoyed the intense excitement of my first encounter. It's too late, now I'm thinking, *"Why didn't I wait?"* I never knew or understood what a waiting period looked like. I thought this was normal. Yea, I heard the conversation about not having sex before marriage, but no one ever had that conversation with me personally. WAIT! WAIT! WAIT! The waiting won't be in vain!

WHAT TO DO WHILE YOU WAIT?

Let's get right to the chase, no sugar coating, no filler! Lock that thing up! Throw away the key to the safety deposit box! Stop letting your emotions drive you into places you have no business going. So what he looked at you! That doesn't mean he's the one for you. So what he asked you for your number! That doesn't mean that you head to the bridal store and purchase your gown. Once you give it up the desire won't go away because it will crave what it's used to. You can't crave for something you've never had! This is not the department where you try things on! I'm so serious! Stop going into every dressing room, trying stuff on, only to find out that it doesn't fit! Now, when they see you coming, you've already tried on everything in the store, they tell you they don't have anything that will fit you! I've literally had friends get mad at me for telling them the truth. If you asked me, I'm going to tell you the truth, so beware!

I had a friend to ask me if it was a good idea to move her boyfriend in her newly purchased townhome that she bought for herself. I said; Nope, not a good idea! She said; we're getting married soon and I want to try it out! She actually said those words! I said; you didn't need to ask me any questions since you already knew the answer. She was a bit upset. He moves in with her and they eventually get married. Okay, that's a good thing right? I get this call that all hell is breaking loose. She says; I never saw this side of him even though we moved in together. My response; Oh yes you did, you thought that saying, "I Do" was going to make him change. That friendship didn't last very long. Why is this important for me to bring up? I've been there! Some of us think that saying those magic words will give us permission to have a fix-it list afterwards. We have the mentality that says; "Now that we're married, I get to point out all of your flaws and help you fix them." We tend to want to fashion and mold our spouse into the thing that we want to see, instead of allowing our Creator, Jesus the Christ to fashion and mold the right one for us.

While shopping, it has become customary to try on things before purchasing them. If we try them on and don't like them, we won't take it home! More than likely, when we purchase an item and we do take it home and it doesn't fit we are quick to return it, nothing wrong with that. Unfortunately, this is how the world is treating marriage. If it doesn't fit, we want to take it back or trade it in! Thus, I believe this is the reason why God told me to wait because He was still fashioning and molding "him" just for me. I thought I'd step in and help out a little bit. Just a little bit! What a mess! We were both immature and not ready. I knew he was the one for me, but the pruning process had not been completed. Therefore, we endured some things that I do not believe we would have encountered if we would have just WAITed!

While you're waiting, stop shopping! You know what I mean! Stop going from store to store (man to man) trying on (having sex) and finding out after you've given away your goods that he isn't the one for you. Allow God to prune, mold, and shape you so that when it is your time, you will already have your stuff in order.

Webster's dictionary defines the word "WAIT" as; *"To stay where one is or delay action until someone arrives or is ready."* This is great! I'll come back to that in a bit. I want to bring your attention to the words associated with waiting: STAY PUT - REST - STOP - HALT - CAUTION! Let's break each of these down.

STAY PUT - Don't move! We can no longer run from place to place in hopes of meeting Mr. Right but instead crash right into Mr. Wrong. Why does this happen? Could it be that Mr. Right is supposed to find you? Just make sure you are where you're supposed to be and no where else. Don't worry, because when it's your time, he will discover you, better yet, he will stumble over you! In the meantime, continue seeking God and ask Him to show you your path!

REST - 1 Kings 8:56 says, *"Blessed be the Lord, that hath given rest unto his people Israel, according to all that he promised: there hath not failed one word of all his good promise, which he promised by the hand of Moses his servant."* Psalm 16:9 says, *"Therefore my heart is glad, and my glory rejoiceth: my flesh also shall rest in hope."* We must rest on the assurance and promises of God! Relax and allow God to do the packaging. I guarantee you, if God puts this together, you won't have to trade it in or take it back. REST IN JESUS, HE ALREADY KNOW WHAT YOUR HEART DESIRES!

STOP - Stop with the bad habits! Are you looking so desperate, walking around with a sign on your forehead that says; I'm single and I'm desperate? No one wants to look like that! Or do you? Although you may be in dire need of having a relationship, be content in the state that you're in and watch what happens. It may be at that very moment that you've decided that you're okay with being alone, that God sends the right one your way. Just like the traffic light, the red stop sign doesn't last forever, it will change to green (GO) eventually. So, you won't have to stay in this state forever, just wait your turn and receive the correct package, with your name on it! It shall be designed and shaped to handle only you! STOP looking at others and their relationships because most of them are fictitious anyway.

HALT - You've been doing things your way so far. You are already going down that path that could possibly destroy you because you are simply not ready. I'm here to command you to "HALT". As your friend and accountability partner, I'm stopping you in your tracks. As a child, we played the game called red light, green light, did you? Before you take another step, I'm stopping you! I'm charging you to come to a complete, abrupt stop! HALT!

CAUTION - Webster defines CAUTION as; care taken to avoid danger or mistakes. WOW! Even when the Lord gives you the green light, you must still use caution. Why? Sometimes we can't see clearly. At times we get so excited that the light has changed from red to green, that we don't proceed with caution. We press on the gas, especially when we're in a hurry to get to our destination. Slow down and use CAUTION! As I mentioned previously, I'm not against love at first sight, all I'm saying is don't marry the man in your mind on the first date. USE CAUTION! Even when you believe He's sent from the

Lord, USE CAUTION again! Seek Him and take heed to what He shows you.

In your singleness why not enjoy your life. Go to the movies with friends, enjoy dinner and shopping. Take a trip, go skiing, go on a singles retreat, take dance lessons, volunteer at a shelter, get out and enjoy your life! Stop moping and wining, hoping that he's going to notice you. If you're depressed and desperate, more than likely that's what you're going to attract! ENJOY YOUR SINGLENESS! YOU'RE GOING TO NEED SOME SELF TIME!

TAKE BACK CONTROL

There is a secret word that no one wants to talk about! Shhhh! Let's not talk about that word! In the Christian community this word is a hush, hush word, although many are secretly engaging in this. Yes, right under our nose. There are many sins in the scripture that we must not commit; even telling lies is a sin, but here I want to specifically talk about the thing that most people struggle with "SEX". SEX is not a bad word! It is designed for married folks! I was introduced to it by a slightly older, handsome gentlemen. I can't say that it was invigorating because I didn't really know what I was doing. Okay, that's enough of that illustration, lol. That excitement didn't come until I met my husband. But it certainly kept me going back. It is crazy how this thing has an invisible string attached to it. It can make you crazy. It can cause you to want to fight for it. Okay, maybe you've never had that experience before, or maybe you have. As a teenager, I would sneak out of the house as if this string was pulling me closer. I found out that I had a habit that I couldn't shake. No one explained to me that once you start, it's almost next to impossible to stop. No one told me that it affects other relationships as well. Yep, I was also secretly active in this area. It was certainly hush, hush, until I found myself in a situation that I couldn't get out of or so I thought. I didn't know how to take control back, it was controlling me! A word that is considered a bad word. It is surely mentioned and talked about openly in the world. Why is this? What is the secret? Some of us were raised to believe that sex was a bad thing. We never even talked about it in the church. Unfortunately, I learned from conversations with my friends and the pressure of what everyone else seemed to be doing. Why the hush? Why can't we get real about something that should be sacred between a husband and wife? We're pretending that it doesn't exist, especially when it comes to our children. Yep, let's be real, they know more than you think.

Why is it important to talk candidly about this subject? Sex is not a bad word! It is a pleasurable time to be enjoyed between husband and wife as ordained by God. It is a sacred gift for married couples, but so many outside of marriage are indulging. What's the secret? What's all the hush about? I can tell you from my perspective that it is a secret because it is "illegal" outside of marriage. We don't want others to see our sin, so we lie or we hide. I didn't understand the concept of sharing these intimate times with my spouse until I was much older. I didn't realize that my indulgence early on would cause infatuation, fantasy and many other things to show up in my life. No one ever warned me or told me if I didn't take control back, it would then control me. The world has this thing all mixed up. Birth control is readily available, and condoms are given away for free in some communities. It paints a picture that says it's okay to have sex before marriage, but no one is having those hard conversations and letting us know why it's wrong and how it can ruin your assigned relationship. If you don't take back control over this area of your life, you may find yourself struggling when your mate arrives. How do I know? I'm glad you asked. Being transparent, I struggled in this area, although I was married, my past experiences caused fantasy to grip me like nothing I could ever have imagined. Even though my husband was right there by my side, it seemed as though I did not have a handle on those thoughts. I began to understand what the definition of a soul-tie was. The problem was, I didn't know how to untie it! Although I tried and tried, it seemed to have a grip on me. It would take Holy Spirit to say to me so clearly, "STOP or BE EXPOSED!" WHEW! There is nothing like the correction of the Father! I had to put that thing up under subjection and be healed. I had to TAKE BACK CONTROL with the help of Holy Spirit of course! Be careful when you meet and marry your mate because all of those emotions and attachments still remain from the old, sometimes the good and the bad. They don't go away by themselves. This type of premarital behavior could cause one to reminisce on the old or what used to be or maybe even what could have been. That word reminisce means; *"To indulge in enjoyable recollection of past events."* Once you connect sexually with your partner it connects you in more than a physical way. Beware!

When you're used to something and then it is no longer there, you tend to long for what you've had a taste of. I have tried to withdraw myself from indulging in sweets and heavy starches, but every now and then they show up in my life and I'm faced with a decision! But if I continue to detox, this will no longer be an issue. We must pray and ask the Lord to take the taste out of our mouth for those things that are not pleasing to Him. Take control by not watching those porn movies and those X-rated movies and picking up those magazines. If you are single and you know you can't handle them, don't do it! Even if you are married, these things can pose problems as well. TAKE BACK CONTROL! You can do it!

TAKE YOURSELF OFF THE MARKET

This may be a controversial subject. You may be thinking that it's impossible to find a mate if you're not on the market or on display in the window. Let me explain! When something is on the market, it gives permission for anybody and everybody to shop, explore, test out, try on, pick over and return. I know you want to be seen and noticed, but you don't have to walk around advertising your singleness and your desperation! You say you're not desperate? Okay, I dare you to walk in assurance that the right one will find you. Remember, he will stumble over you! What happens when you go shopping or to the grocery store? You sometimes notice that the very thing that you want has been picked over. You don't want to be that thing that has been picked over! In some stores, you even get to have a taste of the item that is on sale. No more! I can hear you saying; how will they know I'm single if I'm no longer on the market? Don't worry, the right one will have his eye on you! You may not even see him looking, but he's out there. We don't know where to look anyway. The majority of the times we are looking in all the wrong places. We go to the clubs, bars, etc. I'm not saying that you won't meet your mate at these places, I'm just saying don't make your plans contingent upon you meeting Mr. Right because Mr. Wrong could be in that same place. Your Mr. Right will go before God concerning you and when he shows up you can also go to your Father to confirm if he is the one!

We've all prepared that list of items that we need from the market/grocery store right? What about those items that you pick up that are not on your list? Well, in my case, because I can be so busy at times, I have been known to pick up a brand that I don't recognize, a no name-brand item and those extra items. Now, I'm not saying those brands are bad, I'm just making a point here. I've returned home only to hear my daughter ask me the question, "Did you pay attention to what you were buying or were you in a hurry?" I've even arrived home to discover that I've purchased something that I don't even want anymore. My point here: Take yourself off the market! Stop allowing them to shop around, pick you up, only to return you later on because "they've" discovered that you're not what they wanted. You know you've purchased items in haste also, only to find out it's not what you wanted. You were only available during the shopping spree! The next time they go shopping they will see another name-brand item that they prefer to try out.

You may be asking, "How will they know that you are single if you're off the market?" That's a great question. I'm not saying that you can't go out and have fun and introduce yourself to others, I'm only suggesting that you take yourself off the shelves. In other words, tell them you're not for sale or rent. YOU ARE NOT TO BE PICKED OVER EITHER! If you're going to be on the market just make sure your sign says; "NO RETURNS/NO REFUNDS!" Just having a little fun here! Back to the topic at hand. Why this topic? I believe that if you remove yourself from the "Want Ad" and the stock shelf and become the bride of Christ, your soulmate will have to confront God first. Even the enemy had to confront Christ to seek after Job. Allow him to go to your

Father to get permission to pursue you. Give it time! Don't be so excited about being seen that you forget your standards. Check out the shelf life of most grocery items, they have an expiration date. Oftentimes, those items are disposed of or given away at a discount or lower rate. You may be thinking that your "shelf life" is almost up. Hang in there!

It is customary for the man to go to the father of the bride-to-be and ask for their permission to marry. So, let's not break that tradition! When he first approaches you, go ahead and be bold enough to ask him if he received permission from your Father! Don't be afraid! Just ask him and I can assure you that it will cancel out a lot of the weeds. You know those weeds that keeps popping up in your garden? It doesn't matter how much you put down weed protection fabric, after time, the weeds will come back. In the same manner with relationships, you must be able to be ready to separate the weeds from the good growth! It is critical to be content in your singleness! Trust me, if you're walking around with a desperation sign attached to your back, you're going to certainly attract the wrong thing. Yes, some good may come also, but they will recognize your desperation and flee! If you insist on remaining on the market, just make sure you are watchful and prayerful! Matthew 26:41 says; *"Watch and pray, that ye enter not into temptation: the spirit indeed is willing, but the flesh is weak."*

DON'T JUDGE A BOOK

You've heard the famous statement "Don't judge a book by its cover!" Interesting Facts states: *This phrase was attributed to a 1944 edition of the African journal American Speech: You can't judge a book by it's binding. It was popularized even more when it appeared in the 1946 murder mystery; Murder in the Glass Room by Lester Fuller and Edwin Rolfe.* The phrase "Don't judge a book by its cover" indicates that one should not decide upon something based just on outward appearances. Remember what the Lord told Samuel? 1 Samuel 16:7 *"But the Lord said unto Samuel, Look not on his countenance, or on the height of his stature; because I have refused him: for the Lord seeth not as man seeth; for man looketh on the outward appearance, but the Lord looketh on the heart."* This is exactly where I want to go with this. You see, prior to marriage we often make a long wish list of what we want our mate to look like, sound like and act like. Oh yea, I've been there too. The problem is, we fail to realize that they have a list too! So, while we're looking to the left and to the right for Mr. Right, Mr. Right is passing us by because we don't look like what he may have imagined as well. So, my advice is to put away that long, unrealistic list. Of course, there may be certain things within your moral boundaries that you must have, this could be religious beliefs, etc., but don't limit yourself to all one-hundred things on your list because I can just about guarantee you that he doesn't exist!

Let's talk a bit more about this judgement of the book cover. I would categorize this as two types of books; one so attractive that you can't put the book down and the other, not so flattering, something you'd just pass by. Let's take the book that doesn't interest you, the cover isn't all that captivating or eye catching. Go ahead and put it down and I guarantee you that the right one will pick it up! It's just like the statement "one person's trash is another person's treasure." Keep throwing out what you THINK is trash or unattractive or not your type! By the time they are connected to the right person, they could have you wondering "What in the world did I miss?" I can assure you, when they're grabbed or picked up by the right one, that trash, or so you thought, will no longer look like trash. Let's even reverse this roll; you've examined the book (person) and it looks really attractive, now that look/desire drives you into a relationship with this person, only to find out he's a jerk or worse. The most beautiful thing can sometimes be the most dangerous. I recently took a couple of days to reflect and retreat. My room view was of the beautiful ocean. It was a bit breezy, so the waves were brisk. As I sat in amazement, I began to think, *"How beautiful but how dangerous!"* If you're not a professional swimmer or have some skill you could drown before help arrives unless you have a life jacket. I know you have that shopping list, I mean checklist in hand. Go ahead and admit it! BUT WAIT! Did you check out the water to see how deep it was? Can you swim? Can you handle the waves? My point here is this, stop examining the book cover without knowing what's inside (the heart). Yes, I know you can't see the inward man, but I know a God that can!

Does your shopping list/check list look anything like this?

- ☑ Tall/Short
- ☑ Must be dark-skin/light-skin
- ☑ Must be good-looking
- ☑ Muscular/Sexy
- ☑ Multimillionaire
- ☑ Church-goer
- ☑ No children
- ☑ Owns own home
- ☑ Owns own business
- ☑ Never cursed
- ☑ Never had sex
- ☑ Never made anybody mad
- ☑ Never made any mistakes
- ☑ Must be in leadership
- ☑ Can't own a dog
- ☑ No family drama
- ☑ Must have a degree

What's missing on this list? This list can go on and on. Sometimes we can't even see in front of us because we're too busy mesmerizing on the items on our list. Many are walking around with a check-list in their head and are expecting to bump into what they envision. Shred the list! Remember what we said earlier, he has a list too. Testimony; I'm glad I didn't judge my book by its cover because God changed the pages and it looks so much better than what I saw in the beginning! The things that I thought I needed in the beginning, God gave me so much more. What am I saying? I'm saying, stop limiting God! Don't get me wrong, I know we must use wisdom and discernment because "sometimes" what you see is what you get. I'm not telling you to bring home the homeless man off the street and expect a change. I'm just encouraging you to seek after God because only He can make a perfect match. The question remains; Are we really seeking after God? Are you really? Or are we paving our own path and seeking on our own those things that we need or want? STAY CLOSE TO HIM! Don't trust that friend that claims to be "the perfect match maker." Your Creator is aware of your faults, broken pieces, bent pieces, cracked pieces, shattered pieces, crooked pieces and more. Allow Him to mend every broken piece. Allow Him to mold and shape you so that when He brings your match to you, you'll recognize one another!

DO **YOU** HAVE WHAT IT TAKES?

You're looking for Boaz, but Boaz is looking for Ruth to show up! What does Ruth look like? I'm just curious! What if God doesn't have a Boaz for you, but instead he's a David or a Joshua or a Jonah? Are you still excited about getting married? So many times in relationships we have our "to do list". There is absolutely nothing wrong with that, but we must examine what's on our list as we stated in the previous chapter. In case you don't already have one, I would like for you to develop a new "to do list". This list is not your ordinary, check-off if he meets my criteria list. This list will contain all of the pertinent things that pertain strictly to YOU! Yes, I know it's okay to be specific when you're talking to your Father about what you want in your mate. But, we must remember that He already knows. He knows what we can and cannot handle. He knows our temperament! God does not have to send multiple candidates our way just to see if one fits better than the other. No, that's not God! Although He gives us free will, we want to be certain that He's speaking when it comes to our mate. Getting back to this list. Here are your instructions:

Fold a piece of paper in half. On one half, write down all the negative things about yourself. On the other half, write down all the positive things. I would suggest you engage a close friend, as it may be hard for you to find truth within yourself. I believe this will be a good exercise that will cause you to take an internal look at yourself BEFORE your mate arrives. This will take the focus so much off of the negative things of other people and help you see within! Be honest! If you're lazy, put that down; if you are bossy, put that down; if you have a bit of a nasty attitude at times, put that down. Keep writing! I think it is fair for you to have a list as well, so when Mr. Right arrives, he'll be able to check off his list and declare "CHECK-MATE!" This will help you in the end.

If you're honest with yourself, you'll be able to take a look at your list and ask yourself these questions: Do I have what it takes? Am I ready for the tasks at hand? Am I the right one for him? Am I the perfect match with HIS list? Here's a possibility of his list:

- ☑ Great Attitude
- ☑ Beautiful Personality
- ☑ Loves herself within and it shows on the outside
- ☑ Caring
- ☑ She's already established (working in her area of anointing) *
- ☑ Not lonely
- ☑ Not desperate
- ☑ Approachable

*Most likely this will be the place where he'll stumble over you! So, if you're sitting at home talking about you're lonely and you want a husband, how will he find you if you're not where you're supposed to be? Get up and move! Get up and take care of the Kingdom of God and watch Him take care of your business! That's the promise He made me concerning my household and I'm sticking to it! Let me expound a bit further. So many are simply stagnated and waiting on Mr. Right to show up instead of following their own dreams and visions. Get busy creating; make something, do something, be something, so that when he does arrive, he'll compliment you and you will compliment him. What's happening today? We're waiting for him to show up to complete us. That's not how it is supposed to work. More than likely, if you're complaining about being lonely now, the moment he can't fulfill your needs, you may find yourself right back in that same predicament. Go ahead and fulfill your dreams while you wait!

How do you measure up? Are you ready to take on this type of ministry? If you're not walking out the ministry gift before he arrives, what makes you think you'll be able to handle him? What do I mean? Marriage is ministry! It takes work! It takes work to support, encourage and pray for your spouse. Are you really ready to take on this role? Some of us are self-reliant, self-motivated, selfish, etc. If your attitude is "I go where I want, I do what I want" this isn't going to go well for you. Examine yourself and determine if YOU have what it takes BEFORE HE ARRIVES! Study, read books, talk to successful married couples and learn what it takes. Stop hanging around single, silly woman that will tell you negative things about the relationship that they don't have. Ask yourself this very important question: Am I capable of praying my relationship through during rough times? I know you're not thinking that far ahead, you're just looking at the right now. However, it is crucial to be prepared, so go ahead and practice praying now! You will most certainly need it. How do I know? I'm glad you asked. You have two people coming together, possibly with different backgrounds, beliefs, patterns, habits (good and bad), etc.

Therefore, you will need to be armed with prayer and patience.

Let's have a candid discussion. Here are a few questions that I need you to answer. If your answer is NO to any of these questions, take this time to identify your weak areas.

1. Do you have what it takes to pray when things don't go your way?
2. Do you have what it takes to hush up your mouth when he's made a decision that you may not agree with?
3. Do you have what it takes to keep him in the house and away from the rooftop?
4. Do you have what it takes to work things out without including others?
5. Do you have what it takes to compliment him and not have the desire to stand out all the time?
6. Do you have what it takes to be in the background?
7. Do you have what it takes to put your immediate needs to the side when he needs you to do something for him?
8. Do you have what it takes to please him even when you may not feel like it?

DO **YOU** HAVE WHAT IT TAKES? THINK ON THESE THINGS AND BE PREPARED!

IMPERFECT PUZZLE PIECES

Marriage is like putting two imperfect puzzle pieces together. If you're looking for Mr. Perfect, he won't be found. How do I know? The bible says that there is no perfect one. We're only perfect in the eyes of our Creator while we remain under the blood. Let's take a look at those puzzle pieces. A puzzle piece is specifically shaped and awaiting the touch of its match. Most puzzle pieces are made to fit perfectly together. However, when you've had that puzzle for some time they can get ripped or torn and sometimes they get old and worn. I would consider these imperfect puzzle pieces. It doesn't change its purpose. The puzzle is still considered a puzzle.

"I want you to be perfect" although I'm all jacked up! Many times in our marriages we put so much emphasis on the other person being right and tight but yet we never take a look within. Yes, we will marry the imperfection because it feels good or looks good but once it starts to irritate you it has to go! We have no idea what longevity looks like or what patience looks like. You know you saw those flaws before you stepped to it, didn't you? Some may even be so desperate for the *"plug to fit the socket syndrome"* that their minds are made up to make the imperfect pieces disappear. You especially don't want to get into something only to find out that there is no surge! They forgot to tell you that no matter how you pay the electric bill, the lights still won't come on.

You know what I mean! Don't be fooled! Watch and Pray! I do realize that sometimes life can take a toll on you, so I'm not talking about those types of issues because there's always a workaround. I'm trying to get you to understand that waiting and praying will get you what you need. Stop praying about the size of the puzzle, just make sure it's the right fit!

Not one piece of a puzzle stands alone. Each piece needs to find its mate. But know this, although they are made to fit, sometimes the pieces can be imperfect. They may not fit as snug in some instances. People come in all shapes and sizes (puzzle pieces) and each person has its own personality, thoughts, likes and dislikes. This sometimes poses a problem for some because you may have it set in your mind how your partner should act, live or behave. It is critical to understand that we are all uniquely made. It's not fair for you to pray for something that has been manufactured only to have in mind a remade model. Do you know anyone who bought a perfectly designed car only to be obsessed with making it even better? Well, this is not the way marriage is supposed to be. Yes, there will be some changes, some giving, but don't force your ideas on your mate in order to have them confined to what you think this puzzle should look like. Allow the Manufacturer (Jesus) to do the creating and the making of the puzzle pieces and trust Him to bring your match.

Once the puzzle pieces have met their match, we need to define the things that will keep them together. These are the things that will cause a marriage to last. Although we may mess up in these areas from time to time, we must remember to reconnect because one is dependent upon the other. Here, we will list the most important and discuss them:

Prayer - Prayer is key and essential. Not only is it crucial for your partner to have a prayer life, it is even more critical for you to have already developed one of your own. There will be times when the enemy will come at you to steal, kill and destroy your marriage and the both of you will need to know how to come together to combat the enemy. It is great that you know how to battle but think of how great a territory you could reach if you both were in this thing together.

Communication - Talk to each other! No passive behavior! This is the place of growth and maturity. When you've reached this level, there should be no "I'm not talking to you today" or "I'm just not going to say anything." Again, learn to talk to one another. This is key, even if you think you're silent, you're really speaking. Be careful what you're speaking. Negative body language or giving the silent treatment isn't going to suffice. Now, at times there may be instances where you will need to know when to be silent, but not to purposely make the other person feel inferior nor should you feel as if you're always the one giving in. Grow up! Even if you're the one that has to say; "baby I'm sorry!" They say woman talk too much and men don't talk enough, either way, figure out what works for the both of you and meet each other in the middle.

Trust - Why marry someone you can't trust? Great relationships are built on trust. This is why it is important to get to know the person you are planning to marry. Allow friendships to **GROW**. I'm not against marriage at first sight, I'm just against you thinking that this is the one the moment you set your eyes on them, but then when you say those infamous words "I do" you suddenly realize "you don't after all!" Trust in God with all your heart! Grow your relationship with Christ first, so that your marriage can be healthy.

Worship - Worship the Lord together! Let me tell you ladies what sexy looks like. It looks like a couple worshipping God together! You've got it twisted, you may think sexy has the muscles and broad shoulders, but I'm telling you what lasts a lifetime. It's when a man can worship God with his family. Don't wait to find out when it's too late that the other party doesn't believe in God. If you want to scout out anything beforehand, **check out the worship**!

Respect - *"Esteem for or a sense of worth or excellence of a person, a personal quality or ability, or something considered as a manifestation."* This is key! This will drive how you talk to one another. Just remember that your opinion matters. You may not always agree but as they say; determine to "agree to disagree." RESPECT ONE ANOTHER! You're just two strangers that have come together, trying to get to know one another. It isn't hard, it just takes work! Remember the song; (R-E-S-P-E-C-T)? Part of those lyrics I'd like to concentrate on here; *"find out what it means to me."* Well, that's what this is all about. Find out from each other what the individual need is. Don't be self-centered, only wanting your needs to be met. Consider your spouse! They are a reflection of you!

Sex (often) - Whew! Take the babies out of the room! This is my favorite space in my house. Most people are in love with their fabulous kitchens or bathrooms or walk-in closet. I'm not against those areas, I'm just saying, for me and my spouse, we shall serve one another in the bedroom, or any other place for that matter! This is the place for you to enjoy one another! Be venturous! Explore! Have sex often! Yep, I said it! The marriage bed is undefiled. The Message Bible tells us to guard the sacredness of sexual intimacy between you and your spouse. Don't allow this space to become tainted. Leave those ugly conversations out of the bedroom. Leave those conversations about bills out of the bedroom. Allow this space of intimacy to remain just that! A place that you will commune with one another! So many take this time to argue or fight, I've been there. Instead, use this space to enjoy one another. It's easy to save this space for the negative because it's the last place that we go after a hard or stressful work day. Instead, indulge each other, run bath water, play soft music, light candles and enjoy a fulfilled marriage.

KEEP OR TRADE

"Do you know the saying, Drink from your own rain barrel, draw water from your own spring-fed well? It's true. Otherwise, you may one day come home and find your barrel empty and your well polluted. Your spring water is for you and you only, not to be passed around among strangers. Bless your fresh-flowing fountain! Enjoy the wife you married as a young man! Lovely as an angel, beautiful as a rose — don't ever quit taking delight in her body. Never take her love for granted! Why would you trade enduring intimacies for cheap thrills with a whore? for dalliance with a promiscuous stranger?" Proverbs 5:15-20 Message Bible

Wow! This is plainly stated! Everyone wants to talk about the glitz and glam of the marriage vow, but few want to discuss the reality. This reality is not to prevent one from making that decision or going down this road, it is simply to open up one's eyes to truth. The scriptures let us know that the truth will set us free. Let's open our eyes and receive the truth. We must learn from and study the patterns we frequently see. Go ahead and do an examination. How many couples have you seen in your lifetime that have thrown in the towel after standing before God and committing to their marriage vows? How many? Far too many! We will examine this scripture a bit to get a better understanding of this topic. The definition of the word 'keep' is described as 'retaining possession.' That simply means that the possession remains and is mine. The definition of 'trade' is described as a transaction or buying and selling. Far too many couples get married and decide for whatever reason "this will no longer work!" Our "keeping" power is slim to none. How is it that one minute we are infatuated with one another and the next minute we hate each other? Is that even possible? Oh, yes, it is!

If we are willing to get this concept of commitment, I believe marriages will last and be able to endure the toughest times. We must remember that marriage is like putting two individuals into the boxing rink, both fighting for their right to be right! It is as if you've put two people together, both with a strong sense of "I'm in control!" This isn't going to work! Someone is going to go out for the count. This will only lead to a knockout (failed marriage). A lot of couples want to come into this thing called marriage being the heavy weight champion of the relationship-world! You think you're the best thing since sliced bread, so you expect your trophy. Yes, in the beginning you'll have the goosebumps, the giggles and the shakes! That's all well and good. But what happens the night after thrill wears off? You wake up the next morning or a few days later and the person next to you exposes you to the real "them!" What will you do now? I'm not in any way encouraging premarital sex or taste testing so let's be clear. I want to make sure that you're connected to God and understand His plan for your lives. Make sure that you're in it for the KEEP and that the option is never put on the table for a TRADE! What is the trade? In grade school, we would trade our lunches for what someone else had because theirs "looked" better, when all actually we were given what we needed by our parents. Whenever we saw something that appeared to be better than what we had, we wanted it. This causes us to want to make a trade! And this is what is happening in marriages today. We are too impatient to work on the problems or issues that we experience and believe God that He would keep us in all of our ways. If we (together in marriage) would acknowledge Him, He'll give us the power to stay (keep)!

Go ahead and drink from your own rain barrel and draw water from your own spring-fed well. Get ready to position yourselves in marriage to serve one another in love, stay committed! Get ready to enjoy one another and delight in each other! Never take each other's love for granted! Study one another, explore each other, enjoy each other always!

CONTROL YOUR APPETITE

Are you a foodie? I certainly can be! I love food and the many, many options that are available to us. Have you ever gone to a buffet for lunch or dinner only to find that there are so many options available that you can't quite decide so you get almost everything? I certainly have. In fact, we pile it on our plates as if they are going to run out. I've even piled my plate the first go round to prevent me from having to go back a second time as if that was all right, lol! You know good as well the real problem is simply that we have an issue with controlling our appetite. I complain often about losing weight. It's impossible if you're not going to control what you eat. In this same manner, we must control our appetite when it comes to the opposite sex. Yes, they are all around, like that buffet, all variety and color, size, shape, etc. You're in control of what you put on your plate, which signifies what you can handle. What am I saying here? I'm saying it's okay to have friends of the opposite sex but be careful while you're waiting. Waiting in long lines for the thing that you desire can be a daunting task. It can leave you desperate and by the time you reach the front of the line, you want everything that you see. You want to devour it, indulge in it, overtake it, pile it all on; you know what I mean!

I'm in no way saying that the wait will be easy. I just want to encourage you to get your appetite under control. Whenever God sends your spouse your way, you won't be so desperate and hungry that you devour them before they pop the question. You don't want to look desperate, you simply want to look ready! It will be necessary to put your flesh under subjection. Those feelings of the desire for intimacy is normal. Those feelings of wanting companionship is normal. Those feelings of wanting your needs met are natural. God gave us these feelings, desires and emotions. Make sure you seek the Father concerning your mate! You want someone that can help ignite, start a fire, spark the fire or hey, put out the fire! BUT, until God sends that one to you, tell your flesh to rest until then. I'm not trying to be so deep here, but I would rather see you wait and succeed instead of hastily choosing and failing! Don't worry, you can be recharged! Stop thinking you have to rush into something simply because others are doing it.

It is like going on a diet, tell yourself that you can't have that right now. It won't be forever but right now you're trying to control your appetite. In the meantime, drown yourself in the things of Christ. Remember, walking in your purpose can cause one to find you! And don't worry, you won't lose your appetite. I know it may be complicated trying to control your appetite while others are seemingly enjoying theirs.

Here's my take on the word **CONTROL**:

C - Cast your cares on God. Stop pretending "you are good." You're not good. As a matter of fact, you're tired of waiting. God already knows this, be honest with Him and speak your truth. Let Him know that you're lonelyand tired of waiting. Ask Him to help you with your appetite.

He gave you those desires, so you're not shutting them off, you're just keeping them quiet for now.

O - Own up to your desires, feelings, wants and needs.

N - Never allow yourself to fall for the prey that may not have the same path. Be aware that vulnerability can expose you to the thing that you live to regret!

T - Trust God in all things! Even when picking your mate!

R - Restrain from impulses; those one night stands, thinking it will curb your appetite. It will only result in guilt, shame and failure.

O - Overcome the desire to munch! You know what over snacking does; it causes you to feel guilty and sometimes sick.

L - Listen to those friends that are the closest to you or your family members. Someone that has your heart. More than likely they can see what you don't see. Ask questions! If the person you desire isn't the right fit, your family and close friends will identify that. Yes, God can give you that answer as well, but remember what we discussed earlier! If you've stood in line for a very long time and it's your turn, you can easily put too much of the wrong food on your plate.

1 Corinthians 7:9 (HNV) says; *"But if they don't have self-control, let them marry, for it's better to marry then to burn."* Let's look at this in the Message Bible. "I do, though, tell the unmarried and widows that singleness might well be the best thing for them, as it has been for

me. But if they can't manage their desires and emotions, they should, by all means go ahead and get married. The difficulties of marriage are preferable by far to a sexually tortured life as a single."

YOU CAN CONTROL YOUR APPETITE!

REPEAT OFFENDER CYCLE OF DIVORCE

Tired of trying this thing out and failing? If you've been married before and you don't want to repeat this cycle, this chapter is for you. Many people who have experienced marriage before find it easier to leave or quit when things don't go quite the way they want. Well, how can you avoid becoming a repeat offender? Let's evaluate what went wrong and expose those bad habits so that you won't bring those same issues into your next. I've counseled couples that have remarried only to find out that they are repeating the same old negative cycle. This time around they don't have the drive to stick and stay, instead they are ready to repeat the same cycle of throwing in the towel on their marriage.

This may hit hard, but it is real talk! Stop the madness! First of all, if you've experienced divorce or breakup of any kind, healing needs to take place BEFORE you go into another relationship. Many repeat offenders rush to get married because they feel the "gotta do this now" blues, but few deal with the healing that is needed. Divorce or breakup can be a horrific thing to deal with and can take months or even years to heal. Stop rushing into a new relationship or marriage when you haven't dealt with the old. We are really good with sweeping dirt under the carpet. Yes, I know we've been taught to "get over it" but that alone is not easy nor is it enough. You must first face the pain and deal with it! Take a good look in the mirror and do a serious evaluation of "self" to determine where you failed. Don't look at the other person. In the beginning stages of this, look in the mirror and discover IF/WHERE you went wrong. This is important so that you won't become a repeat offender. What do I mean? If you know that you have a bad attitude that drove your spouse crazy, deal with it, because you will only take that same thing into the new and drive your next crazy, I'm just saying. If you know that you suffer from "I gotta have everything my way," deal with it because trust me, it won't always go your way. If you know that you have the "everything must be perfect" attitude, deal with it. Marriage will not be all about you. I don't like the 50/50 rule, I'd say come whole and healed and you'll be able to give 100/100. That is what makes a relationship. A marriage relationship is simply a correlation to the divine purpose of God. God created Eve because He knew that Adam needed a helpmate. Stop the need to always want things your way! Stop the need to be right! Geesh! I've been there too!

Even if you've made a mistake and it didn't work out, don't stay there. There is hope! If you desire to marry again be careful who you hang out with. Just because you've been hurt, or your marriage didn't work, doesn't give you the right to bash them and put all in the same category. Instead, deal with your pain, deal with your hurt, seek counsel so that you can have a healthy relationship moving forward. There is hope! BUT, you must be honest with yourself and deal with any frailties in your own life, not in the other person. Deal with YOU! Yes, you! I was certainly famous at pointing fingers and asking

God to fix my spouse, not that he didn't need a good fixing, but God chose me to fix instead. Isn't that something! What you mean God? I was asking you to fix him, not me! Really! I had to be willing to have the hard conversations and recognize that we all come short. None of us are perfect! I know this goes against popular belief, but really, we all have flaws. Okay, you don't believe me, try asking a friend the truth! A real friend will tell you that you are mean. A real friend will tell you that you need to smile more! A real friend will tell you that you are selfish! Okay, if you've never heard those words from a friend, come see me, lol! Stop thinking that you have it going on and there is nothing wrong with you. It may not be all your fault, I'm just suggesting that you deal with "self". If you have bad spending habits, seek counsel. You won't make it in marriage if one spouse cheats on their finances when the other one wants to save. Deal with those issues. Go ahead and face them.

The space below is for you to admit your flaws and give them to the Lord. He knows them already; the problem is we try to hide, and we become professional at blaming others. This will cause a marriage to fail! Work together! Pray together! Have fun together! Have lots of sex! Enjoy one another! WHEN issues arise, deal with them together. Stop running to yo mama, yep I said it right. And, stop running outside of your marriage, looking for the opposite sex to talk to. It is a setup from the enemy. Stay home and work things out. Being married for over 30 years, it wasn't always peachy with frosting on top. Sometimes, it was a burnt cake that stunk up the house. I'm just saying. But, we worked things out. Even when I knew I was right, (don't tell my husband), I had to let go and give in. It doesn't mean that you lose your identity or your sense of speech, it just means you're mature and you recognize when to release the rope. Marriage can sometimes seem like you're in a tug of war; who is right and who is wrong. You keep pulling your way and they keep pulling their way. It isn't going to work. Someone is going to get dragged or scarred. Then when you go out in public you look like you've been in a battle, not physical scars, but mental scars. What do I mean? You're not speaking. You're disrespectful to one another. You're yelling at one another! Stop it! No relationship is perfect because there are no perfect people. WORK IT OUT! Get with other couples and stop hanging with your single friends that keep telling you to leave. I PROMISE YOU, IF YOU SURRENDER, GOD CAN WORK IT OUT!

God, I surrender all of my issues to you! Here they are:

_____

_____

_____

_____

_____

DON'T WAIT TO TELL ME

It is said that honesty is the best policy. The scriptures tell us that the truth shall make you free. So, let's start out right. Let the truth be told. There are questions that should be answered BEFORE you say the famous words "I DO!" What better time to have these conversations than on a dinner date. Get to know the person that you are dating or potentially going to marry. Now, I'm not suggesting that you start these questions the first day you meet someone. However, I don't want you spending all of your years with a potential mate only to find out that they are not on the same page, let alone, in the same book. Of course, you'll find that you have differences, that's good. My husband and I are total opposites, but the one thing we have in common is that we both love the Lord. We have different hobbies, we think differently, we act differently, we raise our kids differently, we don't like the same foods, etc., but we know how to come together on common ground when needed. Communication is key! Discover one another early on!

Here are a few questions to get those conversations started. The first thing I would suggest is to do a personal examination to see if you are even marriage material. What do I mean? Sometimes, we search for the thing that we desire but we are nowhere near prepared ourselves. Like Esther, she had a "grooming" process that she had to go through before being presented to the King. What grooming process have you endured to assist you in getting prepared for your King? Don't forget now, he's also looking for Mrs. Right!

Here are some discussion topics. Go ahead, discover your future mate!

Discussion Priorities

Family/Children
Goals: Near Term/Long Term
Religion
Family Values
Hobbies
Travel/Job Career Goals
Finances
Pet Preferences

JUST COMMUNICATE! STUDY! LEARN! EVALUATE! SCOPE OUT!

READY TO SUBMIT?

Ephesians 5:21-25 *"Submitting yourselves one to another in the fear of God. Wives, submit yourselves unto your own husbands, as unto the Lord. For the husband is the head of the wife, even as Christ is the head of the church: and he is the saviour of the body. Therefore as the church is subject unto Christ, so let the wives be to their own husbands in every thing. Husbands, love your wives, even as Christ also loved the church, and gave himself for it."*

God, Husband, Wife, Children! This is God's order. Can you handle this? You want to get married, but are you ready to submit? Are you ready to accept the order that God created? God created man in His image and THEN He created woman to be a helper. Are you sure you are ready for this? Submit is defined as: *To give over or yield to the power or authority of another (comply, bow, obey, agree, resign).* Okay, I know these words look harsh, but we must deal with them. Let's dive right in. When you repeat the vows during the marriage ceremony, the first thing that scares everyone is to hear the word "obey." I believe they've even tried to leave that out or change the wording a bit. I know for me, 30 plus years ago, I was so excited and pressed to say I do, I don't even remember repeating that part. I just realized later on that I had a problem submitting to anyone. Although I don't think I was a problem kid, I surely remember being one that didn't think she needed anyone to tell her what to do.

So, you can imagine how my first year or so of marriage turned out. I mentioned earlier in the book that I didn't have anyone to pattern my life after as far as a successful marriage, so when we had our children, I always put them first. I didn't know any better or so I pretended! Just out of order! Submit! What was that? I didn't even submit to God! Don't judge me! I was unlearned and immature in both my relationship with Christ and my marriage. This is why I highly stress the importance of developing your relationship with Christ FIRST, BEFORE YOU TRY TO DEVELOP A RELATIONSHIP WITH SOMEONE ELSE! Learn how to honor, respect and obey God and you won't struggle with honoring and respecting one another.

All authority comes from God, therefore, we must submit to anyone who is placed in authority over us. In so doing, we submit to God. But, don't get it twisted, submission is not weakness, nor does it grant anyone permission to pull out the doormat! A doormat just lays there, gets stepped on, collects the dirt and doesn't speak up. THIS IS NOT WHAT SUBMISSION MEANS! But what does it actually mean? The problem is we are not taught or clued on what all of this means so we go in with our own preconceived ideas and we mess things up. That word will either scare you away or make you mad. I know! Obey who? Submit to who? Is this word just for the wife? Does it mean that we don't have any say? There are so many questions, but they are never talked about or answered before the big day which leads to arguments and misunderstandings when reality hits. Yield! Yield to Holy Spirit and allow Him to guide the two of you in all that you say and do. Trust me, it won't be hard when Christ is the center! You may have to die to your emotions, old beliefs and feelings, but you will survive. Honor and submission is not one way, it is a two-way street. God is Supreme over all and He requires us to submit to His will. Once we master this, it won't be hard to follow this pattern in your home. Go ahead and submit to the desires of one another!

KEEP YOUR OWN GRASS GREEN

Proverbs 5:1-14 (MESSAGE BIBLE)
NOTHING BUT SIN AND BONES

Dear friend, pay close attention to this, my wisdom; listen very closely to the way I see it. Then you'll acquire a taste for good sense; what I tell you will keep you out of trouble. The lips of a seductive woman are oh so sweet, her soft words are oh so smooth. But it won't be long before she's gravel in your mouth, a pain in your gut, a wound in your heart. She's dancing down the primrose path to Death; she's headed straight for Hell and taking you with her. She hasn't a clue about Real Life, about who she is or where she's going. So, my friend, listen closely; don't treat my words casually. Keep your distance from such a woman; absolutely stay out of her neighborhood. You don't want to squander your wonderful life, to waste your precious life among the hardhearted. Why should you allow strangers to take advantage of you? Why be exploited by those who care nothing for you? You don't want to end your life full of regrets, nothing but sin and bones, Saying, "Oh, why didn't I do what they told me? Why did I reject a disciplined life? Why didn't I listen to my mentors, or take my teachers seriously? My life is ruined! I haven't one blessed thing to show for my life!"

What a warning! You don't want to have any regrets! You must pray and seek God. This is why it is so important to pray for your mate. Is the grass greener on the other side? Stop trying to jump over the fence to see what's on the other side. I was at a church service and one of the ministers there asked me who a particular person was and I told him, but I quickly wondered why he inquired about that person. It dawned on me that his wife was in the same room. I'm not suggesting that he was alluding to anything, but what I can suggest to you (woman), fix yourself up, don't be always frumpy and looking a hot mess! You may argue with me on this one, you may even say that your man should keep his eyes only on you. I'm certainly not suggesting that it is our fault if a man jumps over the fence to check out the grass on the other side. I'm just encouraging you to go ahead and keep your own grass manicured and in perfect condition. Don't worry about the weeds trying to come in. Just keep your stuff sharpened and let your love for your man and how good you treat him be the weed killer, not your mouth or your nasty attitude. Stop complaining that your grass (relationship) is dull or dry. Go ahead and water it, plant seeds, nurture it, cultivate it year-round and pull those weeds within yourself. You won't have to worry about how green someone else grass is because your own will be so appealing. Looking at this in another perspective; stop envying your friends' relationships just because the grass looks green. You don't see those weeds hiding, so you can't judge how good their relationship really is. This also fits in with judging a book by its cover. Don't do it! Stay in your own yard and cultivate it!

Make sure your spouse desires to come home to you! It doesn't matter who cooks the full course meal as long as it is prepared in love. Let me break this down. Remember, we're keeping our own grass green, so here's what your dinner should consist of, my version! Enjoy your appetizer, foreplay (fondling, caressing, kissing, phone calls, cards, flowers, kind words). It is unattractive to argue and fight and disagree all day long and expect your spouse to want to show affection. Relax, Laugh, Enjoy Life! There is enough stress with the cares of the world. Try not to bring those things home. Leave the stressful work life at work. I recognize that there may be times that you come home and may need to digress and talk about issues that you'd faced throughout your day, I'm just saying, don't make this a habit. Yes, it is good to inquire, but if every day is a stressful day, you can make your spouse feel down! Begin to declare your successful day and when you get home you can celebrate over dinner with the main course and dessert!

HAPPILY EVER AFTER

Is there such a thing? Does this place actually exist? Where can we find it? Let's have a reality check right here, right now! There is such a thing, BUT, you have to work at it! There is no magic pill that you swallow or no crystal ball that can make this thing suddenly appear to be real. IT WILL TAKE WORK from the both of you! This is a double-sided job. If you desire a marriage filled with peace and joy and fulfillment, you must become that yourself first. So often we look to other people for fulfillment. What happens when they come up short of your expectation? When we fall short of that illusion, it certainly places unnecessary pressure on your spouse. We MUST seek God for our needs to be met. Happiness is within! It is not contingent upon how other people treat you. As a matter of fact, if happiness exudes out of you, it can become contagious. TRY IT! START SMILING, LAUGHING! ENJOYING LIFE! On the flip side, if you are mean, nasty and always frowning, it's not the other persons' fault, it's your fault!

Let's do some internal (self) house cleaning! Before you invite guests over to your house, you make sure your home is spotless, clean and ready to receive them. If our guests were to open up some of those closets they would find a cluttered mess. Okay, maybe it's just me that hides everything in there. Here, let us take a serious internal look into our secret closets. Go ahead and ask the question; What is in my closet that needs to be disposed of? Some of you may have been single for so long that you have gathered so much stuff that it has now become junk. It is time to clean those closets out. What does your closet look like? Here are some tips:

Get rid of those cluttered spaces. Let me explain. It will be too crowded in your space with your attitude. GET IT TOGETHER! You know you have a bad attitude, but you think finding a spouse will cure that. Nope, it will fall out of that closet sooner than later. I'm not in no way suggesting that you will be on one-thousand all the time. But, if you can grasp the truth that the joy of the Lord is your strength, I believe you will make it. On those days that you feel that your spouse won't understand what you're going through, you won't have a tantrum because they can't relate. You won't walk around mad because you feel as though they can't make you happy. We put so much pressure on one another, but we must realize that our real joy comes from God. It is time to stop looking for love in all the wrong places! Get a grip! Fall in love with the Lord first! He said seek Him and He would give you the desires of your heart!

There was a time in my life when I wanted what I wanted, when I wanted it! It would stress my husband out. I received the best advice. It was; *"Instead of pressuring your husband to understand your need, Ask God!"* How dare they check me, lol! But, I found out that they were right. I was seeking something that I selfishly wanted my husband to provide. Yes, he is the provider of our home, but he is not superman. God is the ultimate supplier of all of our fulfillment. Those empty places that we think our spouses can't fill, Jesus can fill those voids. I explain it this way, for me He lightens the load! What do I mean? Sometimes when I'm trying to get my husband to understand the thing that I'm passionate about may not work in the way I'm presenting it, so instead of nagging him, I pray! Try that! It works!

**HAVE A BLESSED AND
PROSPEROUS MARRIAGE!**

ABOUT THE AUTHOR

Prophetess Cynthia is the founder of Destined2Inspire Ministries where she empowers woman to live purposefully. Her passion is to take the gospel of Jesus beyond the four walls, reaching the lost, those that are depressed and those without hope. She is determined to speak God's truth through her prophetic ministry. She conducts interactive-style workshops that captivates and spark change. These are life-changing experiences where people leave renewed, revived, rejuvenated and free. She travels abroad conducting workshops and speaking engagements. She is the creator of "The Prophetic Birthing Room" where women participate and leave with their babies leaping. Her latest project, "The Be Free Movement" is taking the word of God through theatrics around the world. Most importantly, she loves the Lord!

Prophetess Cynthia is a wife, mother of two beautiful daughters, grandmother of five, workshop instructor, play writer/director, former radio host, prophetic birthing coach, book writing coach, editor, counselor and author of: Live in Your Purpose, Don't Throw in the Towel and I'm Taking My Life Back, You Can Too! She also conducts marriage counseling workshops where marriages are resuscitated. This was birthed out when Holy Spirit reminded her of her initials; C.P.R. She is also an entrepreneur, co-owner of A&C Marketplace Publishing acmarketplacepublish.com. She also assists her family with their entrepreneur endeavors (Rawles Enterprises).

She can be reached via:cynthiarawlesinspires@yahoo.com for speaking engagements, prayer requests, book signing, or for her 6-month coaching program.

COMING THIS FALL!

A couple's game inspired by this book:
"So, You Think You Want to Get Married?"
Created by Prophetess Cynthia Rawles.

www.ingramcontent.com/pod-product-compliance
Lightning Source LLC
Chambersburg PA
CBHW071747040426
42446CB00012B/2489